EXPLORE COLONIAL AMERICA

THE FOUNDING OF AMERICA

Sarah Gilman

Enslow Publishing
101 W. 23rd Street
Suite 240
New York, NY 10011
USA
enslow.com

Published in 2017 by Enslow Publishing, LLC.
101 W. 23rd Street, Suite 240, New York, NY 10011

Library of Congress Cataloging-in-Publication Data

Names: Gilman, Sarah.
Title: The founding of America / Sarah Gilman.
Description: New York : Enslow Publishing, 2017 | Series: Explore colonial America | Includes bibliographical references and index.
Identifiers: ISBN 9780766078765 (pbk.) | ISBN 9780766078581 (6 pack) | ISBN 9780766078703 (library bound)
Subjects: LCSH: United States--History--Revolution, 1775-1783--Juvenile literature. | United States--History--Confederation, 1783-1789--Juvenile literature.
Classification: LCC E208.G55 2017 | DDC 973.3--dc23

To Our Readers: We have done our best to make sure all website addresses in this book were active and appropriate when we went to press. However, the author and the publisher have no control over and assume no liability for the material available on those websites or on any websites they may link to. Any comments or suggestions can be sent by e-mail to customerservice@enslow.com.

Portions of this book originally appeared in the book *Celebrate the Founding of America* by Elaine Landau.

Photos Credits: Throughout book: javarman/Shutterstock.com (tan background), STILLFX/Shutterstock.com (American flag background), Peliken/Shutterstock.com (white stars on blue background); cover, p. 1 SuperStock/SuperStock/Getty Images; p. 4 Pilon/Shutterstock.com; p. 7 Popperfoto/Getty Images; pp. 8, 10, 23 Library of Congress, Prints and Photographs Division; pp. 13, 24 UniversalImagesGroup/Getty Images; p. 17 Public domain/File:Bunker Hill by Pyle.jpg/Wikimedia Commons; p. 19 Universal History Archive/Getty Images; p. 21 MPI/Getty Images; p. 26 GraphicaArtis/Getty Images; p. 27 Victorian Traditions/Shutterstock.com; pp. 30, 41 Hulton Archive/Getty Images; p. 31 rsooll/Shutterstock.com; pp. 32, 34, 37 © North Wind Picture Archives; p. 38 Public domain/National Archives/File:Constitution of the United States, page 1.jpg/Wikimedia Commons; p. 42 Public domain/File:Scene at the Signing of the Constitution of the United States.jpg/Wikimedia Commons.

CONTENTS

The thirteen colonies operated as separate entities. Ultimately, their growing displeasure of the British government made it necessary to band together and fight for independence.

CHAPTER ONE

THE NEED TO TAKE ACTION

The American colonies were growing increasingly unsettled by 1775. Everywhere, people were getting ready for war. Throughout the colonies, military groups called militias had formed. They drilled in open spaces daily. These American colonists were facing a new enemy—Great Britain. This was especially alarming because the colonists were British subjects.

For years, the British government had mainly left the colonies alone. But in 1765, King George III and Parliament began to heavily tax all of the colonies. These taxes were intended to raise funds to pay off debts from the French and Indian War. That war had been fought between the French and the English on American soil. The Stamp Act of 1765 made colonists buy government stamps to be placed on newspapers, playing cards, and many other documents.

EXPLORE THE FACTS

A FAMOUS SLOGAN

The slogan "No taxation without representation" began to be used by the colonists as a protest to taxation. This meant the colonists refused to pay taxes unless they were represented in Parliament.

THE BOSTON TEA PARTY

In 1773, the colonists became really upset about a new tax on tea. On December 16, they let Britain know how they felt. That night a group of Boston colonists tossed 342 chests of British tea into Boston Harbor. The event soon came to be called the Boston Tea Party. People in other American colonies began to fight back against the British as well.

Great Britain was not about to allow this. British troops were sent to Massachusetts and the other colonies. They were there to put down any sign of trouble.

First, public meetings were outlawed. Then, colonists were no longer permitted to elect their own officials. The British also ordered Boston Harbor to be closed. No ships could come in or go out. The harbor was to stay closed until the British were paid for the tea lost in the tea party.

A group of radical patriots boarded a British ship and dumped its cargo overboard. Known as the Boston Tea Party, this bold action captured the attention of the British government.

THE BATTLES OF LEXINGTON AND CONCORD

Angry feelings between Britain and the colonies worsened. At times, fighting broke out between the British soldiers and the colonists' militias. On April 19, 1775, there were armed clashes in Lexington and Concord, Massachusetts.

As tensions mounted, the colonists formed a military in case Britain did not meet their demands. This proved necessary, when shots were fired at Lexington and Concord.

Something had to be done. So on May 10, 1775, leaders from all thirteen colonies met in Philadelphia. The gathering was called the Second Continental Congress. The First Continental Congress had met in September 1774. That Congress had asked Britain to stop its harsh treatment of the colonies, but Britain ignored its demands.

Now it seemed as if a major war might begin. The leaders at the Second Continental Congress had some important choices to make. Their decisions would change life in the colonies for good.

CHAPTER TWO

THE SECOND CONTINENTAL CONGRESS

The delegates to the Second Continental Congress began to arrive in Philadelphia in May 1775. They represented all thirteen colonies. The group would be meeting at the Pennsylvania State House, now known as Independence Hall.

SOME OF THE DELEGATES

One delegate was a thirty-three-year-old Virginia lawyer and plantation owner named Thomas Jefferson. He had been elected to Virginia's colonial legislature (governing body). He was also known to be a very good writer.

Another Virginia delegate was Patrick Henry. Like Jefferson, he was also a lawyer and a member of the Virginia legislature.

The Second Continental Congress met to manage the war effort against Britain. Among its leaders were (from left) John Adams, Robert Morris, Alexander Hamilton, and Thomas Jefferson.

He was a man who said what was on his mind. On March 23, 1775, Henry had given a stirring speech before the Virginia Legislature, asking colonists to take up arms against Britain. His now famous words were "give me liberty or give me death."

George Washington was another Virginia delegate. He owned a plantation and had also been active in Virginia politics. Washington did not care for Britain's rules or taxes.

The delegates from the colony of Massachusetts were an interesting group as well. Among them was a wealthy businessman and active patriot named John Hancock. British officials were anxious to arrest him for treason.

Samuel Adams and John Adams were delegates from Massachusetts, too. The men were cousins as well as patriots. Like Hancock, they had taken part in rebel actions in Boston.

One of the oldest men at the Second Continental Congress was from Pennsylvania Colony. He was sixty-nine-year-old Benjamin (Ben) Franklin. He was already famous for being an inventor, writer, and statesman. He wanted the colonies to break away from Britain.

Caesar Rodney was one of three men from the Delaware Colony. Rodney suffered from cancer of the face. He could have been treated in England, part of Britain. But being a rebel, Rodney would hang if he went there.

These are just a few of the men at the Second Continental Congress. In the months ahead, they would often disagree. Deciding what was best was not always easy to do.

These men had a big responsibility. If Britain refused to treat colonists fairly, they might have to break away from the homeland. That would affect the lives and futures of all the colonists.

CHAPTER THREE

A CONTINENTAL ARMY

May 10, 1775, was the first day of the Second Continental Congress. On that very morning, a New York colonist staged a surprise attack against the British. In a daring raid, a small group of men captured Fort Ticonderoga from the British enemy. The colonists now had the fort's cannons and ammunition. This meant that the fighting against the British had spread to other colonies besides Massachusetts.

Colonists had risen up in Virginia, too. There, Lord Dunmore, the British-appointed governor, had seized most of the colonists' ammunition supply. Patrick Henry called together the local militia. The men forced the governor to return what was taken. The Continental Congress felt forced to act. They knew that the colonies needed an independent army.

As fighting spread to other colonies, it became clear that an organized army was needed. The delegates appointed George Washington (center) commander of the Continental Army.

AN ARMY AND A LEADER

So on June 14, 1775, the Congress created the Continental Army. George Washington was picked to lead the troops. Washington was an experienced and respected soldier. He had fought bravely for the British in the French and the Indian War, the long war fought in America by France and its American Indian allies against Britain.

The delegates believed Washington would be an able leader. And he agreed to be the new army's general. But Washington refused to accept a salary. Washington believed in what he was doing. That was payment enough for him.

EXPLORE THE FACTS

GENERAL WASHINGTON

George Washington was an excellent leader of the Continental Army. It is surprising to know that he hated fighting. He preferred to spend time on his farm, growing crops.

George Washington faced a difficult task ahead. His soldiers were untrained. Some were as young as fifteen. Many had never fought before.

The Continental Army did not have enough weapons or ammunition either. Often there were barely enough food or uniforms. Some men did not even have boots to march in. Yet Washington was determined not to fail.

CHAPTER FOUR

AN IMPORTANT BATTLE

Washington left Philadelphia and headed for Boston as soon as he could. He was to take over the troops there. Yet even before he arrived, there was more trouble. By mid-June the British had sent still more troops to Boston. Warships filled with British soldiers were to help the British troops already there.

THE BATTLE OF BUNKER HILL

The colonists were determined to fight back. On the night of June 16, 1775, more than 1,200 militiamen took their places on a hill just north of Boston. While it was dark they dug trenches. They made a fort out of thick walls of dirt.

Early the next morning the British saw what the militia had done. They did not want the enemy to fire down on them with their cannons. So the British decided to take the hill. It seemed easy enough to do. The British had many more men. They were also far better armed.

The militiamen were extremely short on bullets. So every bullet had to count. When aiming at the British, the men were told by one militia leader: "Don't fire until you see the whites of their eyes."

The fighting raged on all day. Twice the British tried to charge up the hill and the militiamen beat them back. The British finally made it on their third try.

EXPLORE THE FACTS

THE WRONG HILL

The Battle of Bunker Hill actually took place on Breed's Hill. The army mistakenly thought the battle site was Bunker Hill, a nearby hill. So the battle was actually named for the wrong hill.

NOT A TOTAL LOSS

By then the militiamen were out of ammunition. But they were not ready to give up. They fought their enemy in hand-to-hand combat. They hit the British with the butts of the rifles. They threw rocks at them, too. Nevertheless, in the end, the rebels were forced to retreat, or run away, from the battle.

Even though the British were the victors on Breed's Hill, they suffered tremendous losses. This was enough to encourage the militiamen that they could stand up to the British Army.

The British won the costly victory. Of nearly 2,400 British soldiers, about half were either wounded or killed.

The colonists were proud of themselves. They had taken a toll on the British forces. The Battle at Bunker Hill, as it came to be called, would never be forgotten.

About three weeks later, General George Washington arrived in Boston. He saw that these men had spirit. Now he had to turn these farmers into a real army.

CHAPTER FIVE

ONE LAST CHANCE

The patriots had engaged in isolated battles with the British. However, it seemed as if a full-blown war with Britain was coming.

The colonies wanted to avoid further fighting if they could. On July 6, 1775, the Second Continental Congress issued an important statement known as "A Declaration of the Causes and Necessity of Taking up Arms." It warned Britain that the colonists would fight to defend their rights and liberty.

A DIFFERENCE OF OPINION

While the delegates had come together to draft the statement, they often disagreed on exactly what to do. They had many long, heated arguments. Even on the hottest summer days, the windows at the statehouse remained shut. The delegates did not want people to hear them shouting.

Some delegates, like Samuel Adams, thought the colonies should declare their independence. Battles had already been fought and American lives lost. Yet others, like the lawyer John Dickenson from the Pennsylvania Colony, felt differently. Dickinson and some others hoped to work things out with Britain.

John Hancock, a delegate from Massachusetts, served as president of the Continental Congress. The delegates could not agree on whether the colonies should fight for independence.

These delegates argued that Britain remained an important trading partner. Many businessmen in the colonies sold goods to Britain. That was how they made their living. These delegates also like the idea of being under Britain's protection. After all, Britain was one of the most powerful nations in the world.

EXPLORE THE FACTS

AMBASSADORS ABROAD

The Congress sent ambassadors to other countries to ask for help in the struggle against the British. They asked for money, men, weapons, and ships. Perhaps the most successful of these ambassadors was Benjamin Franklin.

A PETITION TO KING GEORGE

The differing views of the delegates existed among average citizens in the colonies as well. So the Second Continental Congress decided to move ahead slowly and cautiously. On July 8, 1775, it sent a petition (a request signed by many people) to King George III, asking for an end to Britain's unjust treatment of the colonies. But the King refused to read the petition. He had his own plans for the colonies. These included using force to crush a rebellion.

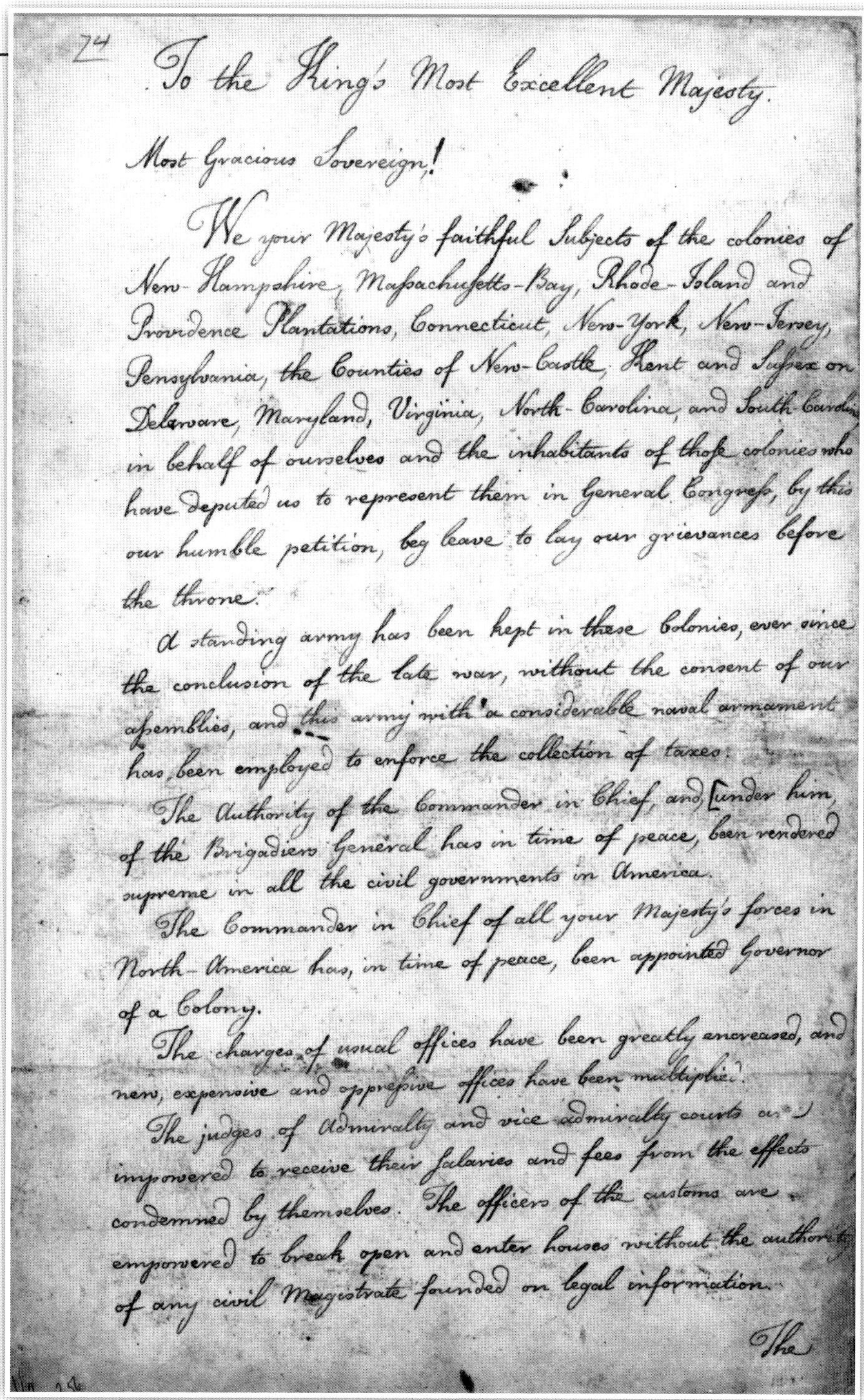

24

To the King's Most Excellent Majesty.

Most Gracious Sovereign!

We your Majesty's faithful Subjects of the colonies of New-Hampshire, Massachusetts-Bay, Rhode-Island and Providence Plantations, Connecticut, New-York, New-Jersey, Pensylvania, the Counties of New-Castle, Kent and Sussex on Delaware, Maryland, Virginia, North-Carolina, and South-Carolina in behalf of ourselves and the inhabitants of those colonies who have deputed us to represent them in General Congress, by this our humble petition, beg leave to lay our grievances before the throne.

A standing army has been kept in these Colonies, ever since the conclusion of the late war, without the consent of our assemblies, and this army with a considerable naval armament has been employed to enforce the collection of taxes.

The Authority of the Commander in Chief, and, under him, of the Brigadiers General has in time of peace, been rendered supreme in all the civil governments in America.

The Commander in Chief of all your Majesty's forces in North-America has, in time of peace, been appointed Governor of a Colony.

The charges of usual offices have been greatly encreased, and new, expensive and oppressive offices have been multiplied.

The judges of Admiralty and vice admiralty courts are impowered to receive their salaries and fees from the effects condemned by themselves. The officers of the customs are empowered to break open and enter houses without the authority of any civil Magistrate founded on legal information.

The

The delegates sent an "Olive Branch petition" to King George. This letter listed the colonies' grievances and proposed solutions. They hoped to avoid further fighting.

CHAPTER SIX

PREPARING FOR WAR

The fighting continued on through the fall and cold winter months. By the spring of 1776, there had been more fighting in Massachusetts, as well as Virginia.

COMMON SENSE

The colonies were full of Loyalists, or Tories, who remained loyal to King George and did not want to break away from Britain. More colonists, however, had begun to favor independence. This was largely due to an influential pamphlet, or booklet, called *Common Sense*. It was written by a former British tax collector named Thomas Paine.

Paine believed that people should govern themselves. In *Common Sense*, Paine urged the colonists to make a final break with Britain. He believed that the colonies could be a shining example of a free nation. *Common Sense* became a best seller and was read by many colonists.

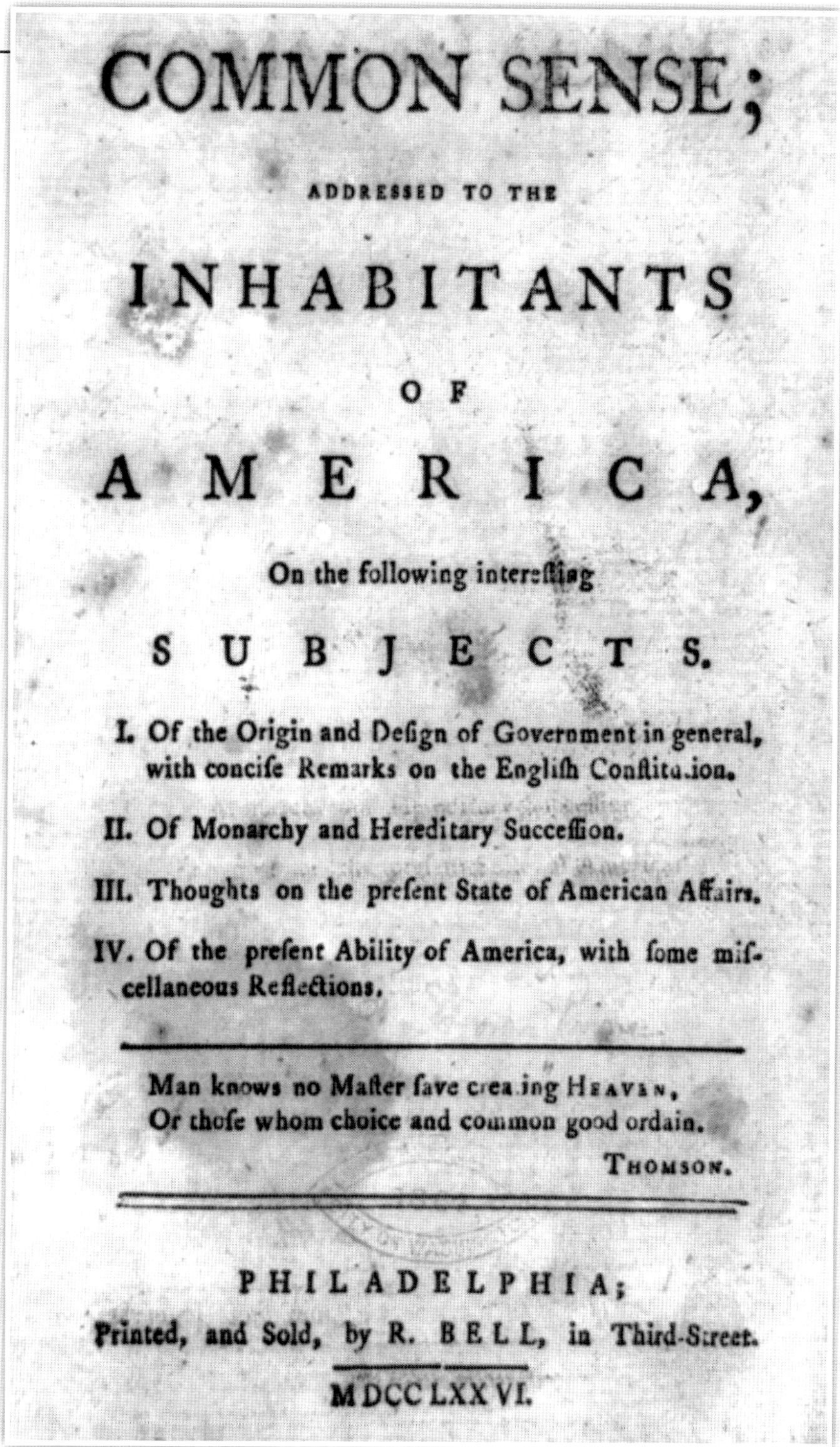

COMMON SENSE;

ADDRESSED TO THE

INHABITANTS

OF

AMERICA,

On the following intereſting

SUBJECTS.

I. Of the Origin and Deſign of Government in general, with conciſe Remarks on the Engliſh Conſtitution.

II. Of Monarchy and Hereditary Succeſſion.

III. Thoughts on the preſent State of American Affairs.

IV. Of the preſent Ability of America, with ſome miſcellaneous Reflections.

Man knows no Maſter ſave creating HEAVEN,
Or thoſe whom choice and common good ordain.

THOMSON.

PHILADELPHIA;
Printed, and Sold, by R. BELL, in Third-Street.

MDCCLXXVI.

Thomas Paine's ***Common Sense*** became incredibly popular. The pamphlet influenced many colonists to support independence.

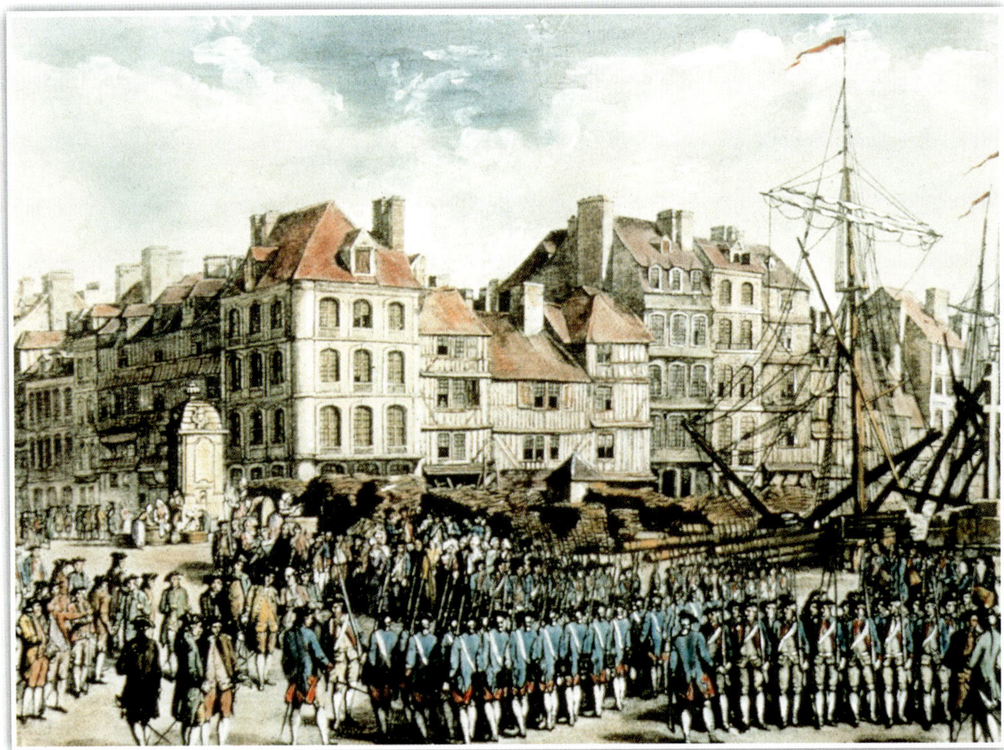

Mercenaries from Hesse (part of modern Germany) arrived in America to fight on the side of Britain in the Revolutionary War.

KING GEORGE BOLSTERS BRITAIN'S ARMY

More delegates to the Second Continental Congress were beginning to think the same way. King George III had continued to send troops to the colonies. He hired about 30,000 Hessian (German) soldiers to fight against the colonists. They were fierce fighters.

He also urged American Indians to fight on Britain's side. The Indians were ready to do so. They were angry with the colonists for taking their land. The colonists would have to band together in the coming months. They may even need to find some help of their own.

CHAPTER SEVEN

A DECLARATION OF INDEPENDENCE

Meanwhile, the colonists were still supporting their cause. But it needed a resolution. By May 1776, fighting with Britain, which we call the American Revolution, had continued for more than a year. The Continental Congress had been in session for a year as well. Yet the delegates continued to argue about becoming free from Britain.

NOT READY TO VOTE

Then, on June 7,1776, delegate Richard Henry Lee of Virginia made a bold move. He suggested that they vote to see how many delegates were ready to declare independence.

John Adams led the charge for colonial independence from Britain. Adams would go on to become the second president of the United States.

Delegates from seven of the thirteen colonies were ready to vote. However, the delegates from Delaware, Maryland, New Jersey, New York, Pennsylvania, and South Carolina were not.

The Congress decided to putt off an official vote until July 2. That way the delegates could write to their home colonies. These men wanted to be sure they did what the people wanted.

JEFFERSON SITS DOWN TO WRITE

In the meantime, Congress prepared itself for what might happen. It put together a committee to draw up a Declaration of Independence. The writing committee included Ben Franklin from Pennsylvania and John Adams of Massachusetts. Roger Sherman from Connecticut and Robert R. Livingston of New York were to help, too. However, the committee member who would actually do most of the writing was a Southerner. It was none other than Thomas Jefferson.

Jefferson got up every morning at dawn to write. Then, after being in Congress all day, he would write at night, too. He worked at his desk in his small rented room in downtown Philadelphia.

Virginia delegate Thomas Jefferson took on the task of drafting the Declaration of Independence alone. The important document was reviewed, edited, and improved upon, however, by delegates Ben Franklin and John Adams.

Jefferson wanted the declaration to be perfect. It had to stand for what was in the hearts and minds of the people.

After about two weeks, he was finally ready to show his work to Ben Franklin and John Adams. They made still more changes to it. The delegates had not voted yet, however. No one knew for sure if they would even need a Declaration of Independence.

CHAPTER EIGHT

THE VOTE FOR INDEPENDENCE

The time was finally ready for the delegates in Philadelphia to vote. Would they vote for independence? The vote was planned for July 2, 1776.

The day before, the delegates took a trial vote to see where everyone stood. Pennsylvania delegate John Dickenson spoke before the vote was taken. He did not feel the colonies were for independence. Next, John Adams spoke. He urged the delegates to break with Britain.

A SPLIT

In the end, the vote was split. Delegates from nine colonies chose independence. South Carolina and Pennsylvania cast their ballots against it. The New York delegates did not vote at all. They were still waiting for advice from home.

The delegates prepared documentation for the Declaration of Independence even though the vote for independence had not yet been held.

The Delaware vote was split. One delegate wanted independence while another did not. Caesar Rodney was the third Delaware delegate. But he was not in Philadelphia. There had been trouble in his colony and he had gone back to help. Yet, Rodney favored independence. He could break the tie vote.

A messenger was sent to Delaware to fetch Caesar Rodney. Rodney hopped on his horse and headed for Philadelphia. That night he rode eighty miles through a rainstorm. He wanted to be there for the final vote.

This Delaware quarter celebrates the heroic ride of Caesar Rodney. The Delaware delegate embarked on a long and treacherous journey to vote. Rodney's vote would break the colony's tie.

ONE STEP CLOSER

The delegates voted again late the next day. Their vote on July 2, 1776, was for freedom. Caesar Rodney broke the Delaware tie. South Carolina and Pennsylvania now voted for independence, too. Their delegates had been convinced by others to change their vote.

Following the vote, Congress made some further changes to the Declaration of Independence. Then on July 4, 1776, the delegates officially adopted, or accepted, the document.

EXPLORE THE FACTS

THOMAS JEFFERSON

Thomas Jefferson continued to serve the public for much of his life. He was elected Governor of Virginia before serving as Secretary of State. In 1801, he became the third president of the United States.

This illustration depicts the signing of the Declaration of Independence by the delegates. The first copy of the document was signed only by John Hancock and distributed as a broadside. The rest of the delegates signed another copy of the document at a later date.

CHAPTER NINE

THE UNITED STATES OF AMERICA

After the delegates formally adopted the Declaration of Independence, copies of the document were quickly printed and sent out to all the colonies.

The declaration was read to gathered crowds of anxious colonists. When it was read, the people cheered. The thirteen colonies would soon be thirteen states.

ARTICLES OF CONFEDERATION

But the story does not end here. Declaring their independence was the easy part. The colonists still had to win the war with Britain. If they won, they would need a plan for a new government.

The Declaration of Independence was printed and distributed to the colonies to be read in public gathering places. This scene shows a reading at Boston's Old State House.

On July 12, 1776, the Second Continental Congress formed a committee to work on a plan. They wrote a document known as the Articles of Confederation. These were the rules that the new government was supposed to follow.

AN END TO THE WAR

Meanwhile, the American Revolution continued. The colonial army fought long and hard. Many soldiers lost their lives. Finally the British surrendered to Washington on October 19, 1781, after losing a battle at Yorktown, Virginia.

That was the last major battle of the war. Over the next two years, there would be small clashes in some areas. However, the colonists had clearly won the war.

The British and the Americans signed a peace treaty on September 3, 1783. In January of the following year, Congress approved it. At last, the United States was truly an independent nation.

A FLAWED DOCUMENT

Now the new nation needed a government that would last through the years. While the Articles of Confederation seemed like a good idea, it was not. Under it, each state remained fully independent. It was as if they were thirteen different nations.

The Articles gave the national government too little power. It could not call up troops or get money from the states without the states' permission. The new government could not even print paper money.

CHAPTER TEN

A NEW CONSTITUTION

The delegates were concerned that their new government was not strong enough. They decided they needed to revise the Articles of Confederation they had created. In May 1787, delegates met in Philadelphia to improve the document.

However, they decided to create an entirely new plan for a government instead. This meeting came to be known as the Constitutional Convention. The plan designed there became the basis for the United States Constitution.

RATIFICATION

The Constitution gave the country a strong national government. Yet the states still had many rights and powers. The Constitution also made sure that the government represented the people. They would choose delegates to represent them.

The delegates at the Constitutional Convention met for the last time on September 17, 1787. That day the Constitution was read and signed. Now it was up to the states to ratify, or approve. the Constitution. Delegates from each state would either vote for it or against it.

Those in favor of the Constitution were called Federalists. They argued that a strong national government was needed. Those against approval of the Constitution were known as anti-Federalists. These included Patrick Henry. He felt that the Constitution gave the government far too much power. Samuel Adams and John Hancock were also anti-Federalists.

In the end, however, the Federalists won. Rhode Island became the last state to approve the Constitution in 1790. It then became the law of the land.

Ben Franklin also was an accomplished musician and scientist. His experiments with electricty are legendary.

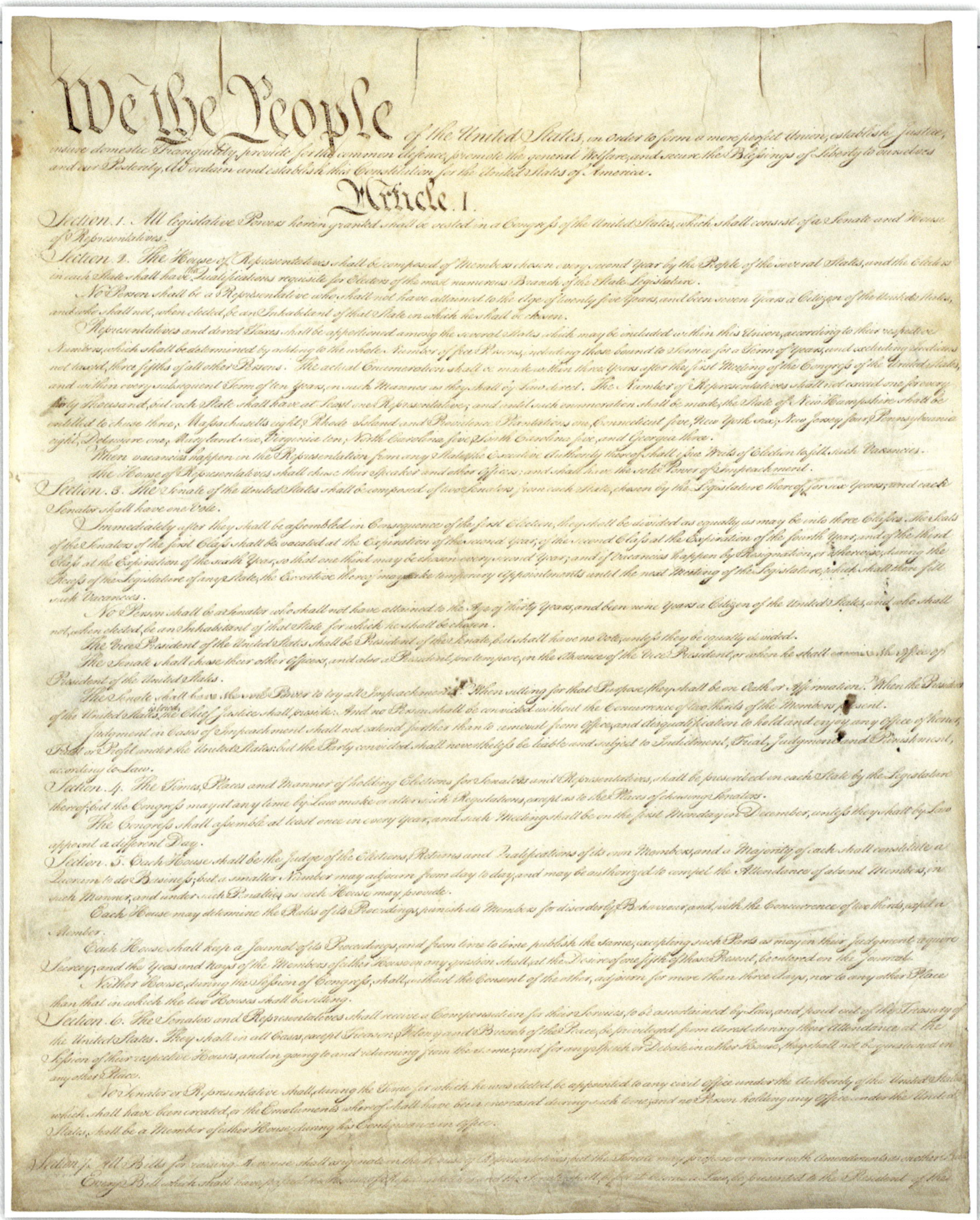

We the People of the United States, in Order to form a more perfect Union, establish Justice, insure domestic Tranquility, provide for the common defence, promote the general Welfare, and secure the Blessings of Liberty to ourselves and our Posterity, do ordain and establish this Constitution for the United States of America.

Article. I.

Section. 1. All legislative Powers herein granted shall be vested in a Congress of the United States, which shall consist of a Senate and House of Representatives.

Section. 2. The House of Representatives shall be composed of Members chosen every second Year by the People of the several States, and the Electors in each State shall have the Qualifications requisite for Electors of the most numerous Branch of the State Legislature.

No Person shall be a Representative who shall not have attained to the Age of twenty five Years, and been seven Years a Citizen of the United States, and who shall not, when elected, be an Inhabitant of that State in which he shall be chosen.

Representatives and direct Taxes shall be apportioned among the several States which may be included within this Union, according to their respective Numbers, which shall be determined by adding to the whole Number of free Persons, including those bound to Service for a Term of Years, and excluding Indians not taxed, three fifths of all other Persons. The actual Enumeration shall be made within three Years after the first Meeting of the Congress of the United States, and within every subsequent Term of ten Years, in such Manner as they shall by Law direct. The Number of Representatives shall not exceed one for every thirty Thousand, but each State shall have at Least one Representative; and until such enumeration shall be made, the State of New Hampshire shall be entitled to chuse three, Massachusetts eight, Rhode Island and Providence Plantations one, Connecticut five, New York six, New Jersey four, Pennsylvania eight, Delaware one, Maryland six, Virginia ten, North Carolina five, South Carolina five, and Georgia three.

When vacancies happen in the Representation from any State, the Executive Authority thereof shall issue Writs of Election to fill such Vacancies.

The House of Representatives shall chuse their Speaker and other Officers; and shall have the sole Power of Impeachment.

Section. 3. The Senate of the United States shall be composed of two Senators from each State, chosen by the Legislature thereof for six Years; and each Senator shall have one Vote.

Immediately after they shall be assembled in Consequence of the first Election, they shall be divided as equally as may be into three Classes. The Seats of the Senators of the first Class shall be vacated at the Expiration of the second Year, of the second Class at the Expiration of the fourth Year, and of the third Class at the Expiration of the sixth Year, so that one third may be chosen every second Year; and if Vacancies happen by Resignation, or otherwise, during the Recess of the Legislature of any State, the Executive thereof may make temporary Appointments until the next Meeting of the Legislature, which shall then fill such Vacancies.

No Person shall be a Senator who shall not have attained to the Age of thirty Years, and been nine Years a Citizen of the United States, and who shall not, when elected, be an Inhabitant of that State for which he shall be chosen.

The Vice President of the United States shall be President of the Senate, but shall have no Vote, unless they be equally divided.

The Senate shall chuse their other Officers, and also a President pro tempore, in the Absence of the Vice President, or when he shall exercise the Office of President of the United States.

The Senate shall have the sole Power to try all Impeachments. When sitting for that Purpose, they shall be on Oath or Affirmation. When the President of the United States is tried, the Chief Justice shall preside: And no Person shall be convicted without the Concurrence of two thirds of the Members present.

Judgment in Cases of Impeachment shall not extend further than to removal from Office, and disqualification to hold and enjoy any Office of honor, Trust or Profit under the United States: but the Party convicted shall nevertheless be liable and subject to Indictment, Trial, Judgment and Punishment, according to Law.

Section. 4. The Times, Places and Manner of holding Elections for Senators and Representatives, shall be prescribed in each State by the Legislature thereof; but the Congress may at any time by Law make or alter such Regulations, except as to the Places of chusing Senators.

The Congress shall assemble at least once in every Year, and such Meeting shall be on the first Monday in December, unless they shall by Law appoint a different Day.

Section. 5. Each House shall be the Judge of the Elections, Returns and Qualifications of its own Members, and a Majority of each shall constitute a Quorum to do Business; but a smaller Number may adjourn from day to day, and may be authorized to compel the Attendance of absent Members, in such Manner, and under such Penalties as each House may provide.

Each House may determine the Rules of its Proceedings, punish its Members for disorderly Behaviour, and, with the Concurrence of two thirds, expel a Member.

Each House shall keep a Journal of its Proceedings, and from time to time publish the same, excepting such Parts as may in their Judgment require Secrecy; and the Yeas and Nays of the Members of either House on any question shall, at the Desire of one fifth of those Present, be entered on the Journal.

Neither House, during the Session of Congress, shall, without the Consent of the other, adjourn for more than three days, nor to any other Place than that in which the two Houses shall be sitting.

Section. 6. The Senators and Representatives shall receive a Compensation for their Services, to be ascertained by Law, and paid out of the Treasury of the United States. They shall in all Cases, except Treason, Felony and Breach of the Peace, be privileged from Arrest during their Attendance at the Session of their respective Houses, and in going to and returning from the same; and for any Speech or Debate in either House, they shall not be questioned in any other Place.

No Senator or Representative shall, during the Time for which he was elected, be appointed to any civil Office under the Authority of the United States, which shall have been created, or the Emoluments whereof shall have been encreased during such time; and no Person holding any Office under the United States, shall be a Member of either House during his Continuance in Office.

Section. 7. All Bills for raising Revenue shall originate in the House of Representatives; but the Senate may propose or concur with Amendments as on other Bills.

Every Bill which shall have passed the House of Representatives and the Senate, shall, before it become a Law, be presented to the President of the

After coming to the realization that the Articles of Confederation was not sufficient as supreme law, a Constitutional Convention met to create a new constitution. This document, along with additional amendments, has served America for more than 200 years.

THE BILL OF RIGHTS

Only a year after it was approved by the states, however, the Constitution was changed. In December 1791, the Bill of Rights was added. The Bill of Rights states the Americans have certain rights that cannot be taken away from them.

Yet the Bill of Rights did not protect everyone. Slaves in America had no rights. Under the Constitution, representation in the government was based on the number of people in a state. A slave only counted as three-fifths of a person.

Over the years, the Constitution would be changed again and again. Slavery was outlawed in 1865. African Americans were later guaranteed the same rights as others in the twentieth century.

CHAPTER ELEVEN

LET FREEDOM RING

Today the Constitution remains an important document for all Americans. It protects our liberty and way of life. The delegates did what they set out to do. The proof is in the freedom we enjoy today.

THE PRICE PAID

The men involved in the formation of the United States of America were true patriots. They provided the leadership their country needed at the time.

However, in many cases, these men paid a high price for declaring freedom. Before the end of the war, the British often searched for signers of the Declaration of Independence. They wanted to make examples of them.

Members of the Constitutional Convention signed the new US Constitution. Though most delegates believed they would never agree on every point, they were satisfied with their work.

Some signers had their homes destroyed. Many lost all their money. Others had to hide themselves and their children to escape capture by the British. A few were sent to prison and some were even killed during the war.

Yet in the end, all of these men were heroes. They helped create a country based on freedom. Also, they stood up for what they believed in. The new nation would grow strong because of their courage.

George Washington was a widely respected leader and one of the most important founding fathers. He served as the Continental Army's commander, was unanimously elected to the presidency twice, and presided over the Constitutional Convention.

EXPLORE THE FACTS

GEORGE WASHINGTON

George Washington became the nation's first president. He was elected in 1788 and again in 1792. Washington died at the age of sixty-seven on December 14, 1799.

TIMELINE

1765

The Stamp Act forces colonists to buy government stamps to place on many items.

1773

December 16—The Boston Tea Party takes place on December 16.

1774

September—The First Continental Congress opens.

1775

March 23—Patrick Henry gives a stirring speech before the Virginia legislature.

April 19—The battles at Lexington and Concord are fought.

May 10—The Second Continental Congress opens; the colonists capture the British-controlled Fort Ticonderoga.

June 16—The battle on Breed's Hill (later know as the Battle of Bunker Hill) takes place.

July 6—The Second Continental Congress issues the statement known as "A Declaration of the Causes and Necessity of Taking up Arms."

July 8—The Second Continental Congress sends their demands to King George III.

1776

June 7—Richard Henry Lee of Virginia suggests that the delegates of the Second Continental Congress vote to see where they stand on the question of independence.

July 1 and 2—The Second Continental Congress votes for independence.

July 4—The Second Continental Congress officially adopts the Declaration of Independence.

1781

March 1—The states approve the Articles of Confederation.

October 19—The British surrender to General George Washington at Yorktown, Virginia.

1783

September 3—The British and Americans sign a peace treaty.

1787

May—The Constitutional Convention meets.

September 17—The US Constitution is signed.

1790

Rhode Island becomes the final state to ratify or approve the Constitution.

1791

December—The Bill of Rights is added to the Constitution.

GLOSSARY

DELEGATES—People sent to meetings to represent others.

LEGISLATURE—A government body that makes laws.

MILITIA—A group of citizens used in emergencies who are trained to fight.

OUTLAW—To forbid something by law.

PARLIAMENT—The British section of the government that makes laws.

PATRIOT—Someone who loves and defends his or her country.

PETITION—A document, signed by many people, asking those in power to change something.

RATIFY—To approve or adopt a document or piece of legislation.

SEIZE—To take or capture a person or property.

STATESMAN—An individual skilled in the ways of government.

SUBJECT—A person under the control or authority of a monarch.

TAX—Money paid by people to support the government.

TREASON—Betrayal of one's country.

FURTHER READING

Adamson, Thomas K. *The American Revolution.* Mankato, MN: The Child's World, 2015.

Burgan, Michael. *United States of America.* New York: Children's Press, 2014.

Cunningham, Kevin. *The Boston Tea Party.* Danbury, CT: Children's Press, 2013.

Gosman, Gillian. *George Washington.* New York: PowerKids Press, 2011.

Krensky, Stephen. *The Constitution.* New York: Marshall Cavendish Benchmark, 2012.

Ribke, Simone T. and Nanci Reginelli Vargus. *Thomas Jefferson.* New York: Children's Press, 2014.

Shea, John M. *The Declaration of Independence.* New York: Gareth Stevens Publishing, 2014.

FOR MORE INFORMATION

BEN'S GUIDE TO THE US GOVERNMENT FOR KIDS—BENJAMIN FRANKLIN

bensguide.gpo.gov/

Learn about Ben Franklin's work as a printer, librarian, inventor, and statesman.

THE BOSTON TEA PARTY SHIP & MUSEUM

www.bostonteapartyship.com

Visit the site of the museum that recreates the Boston Tea Party for visitors. Don't miss the replicas of the ships.

THE DECLARATION OF INDEPENDENCE

www.ushistory.org/declaration

Check out this website to learn about the Declaration of Independence and those who signed it.

INDEX